Stargazing from Hell

by

BRIAN GREENWOOD

© 2012-2018 by Secret Chord Music Group, Inc. All Rights Reserved.

Storm	1
The Shadow Lover	2
To Cover Blue Miles	3
Into Your Tides	4
Trunk	5
Secrets and Sacred	6
Until Flesh Becomes Bone	7
Off to Grey	8
Consider	9
To Lend	10
Eternity's Chains	11
Don't Pretend	12
Library	13
Brother	14
The Island of Everywhere	15
Sun is Mine	16
Birth Yet Anew	17
Synchronicity	18
Birth	19
Far Below	20
Ballerinas and Whiskey	21
More Than Black	22
The Devil's Inscription	23
Comes Yet Still	24
Vehement Vision	25
Now	26
Rolling Hills of Azure	27
Banter	28
Left	29
Avenue	30
Flying	31
From the Mountain	32
Seems Unsettled	33
Promised to Whom	34

And It's Over	35
Drenched	36
And to...?	37
Is the Tragedy	38
Atop Married Hill	39
Eager Soldiers	40
This Cage	41
The Ghost and the Insane	42
Behind the Face	43
This Empty Room with You	44
Pink Moons and Blue Lagoons	45
Sailing	46
Wondering	47
And Just Run	48
Meet Again	49
Once Were Far	50
Shopping List	51
Nothing Saved	52
Waiting	53
What Garden	54
On Owning Sunset	55
A Scene at Riverside	56
The Sick Men	57
Stones	58
Between Her Legs	59
Red Sun	60
So	61
Too Real	62
Nearing Insanity	63
Left Alone	64
Let Her	65
Leaving Only Time	66
Wave	67
Everyone's A Whore	68

The Lonely People	69
Id	70
Quiver & Yonder	71
Nights & Fire	72
An Even Number	73
Whatever	74
Still Sour	75
When	76
Eternal Sea	77
Lies Still	78
Morning View	79
Sweet Taste	80
Flames	81
Building Skies	82
And It's Over	83
Armada	84
Certain Pain	85
The Death of Dawn	86
The Outsiders	88
A Virgin's Thighs	89
Faces Now in Mirrors Wade	90
Self-Affair	91
Dig It	92
Sepulcher	93
When What Wake	94
Lost Time	95
The Spy	96
Stealing Repose	97
Clocks	98
Your Death	99
Who?	100
Sunday Night in Hollywood	101
Ritual	102
For A Time	103

That Was Then	104
Standing By	105
Such Affairs	106
Creeping	107
She	108
They Kept Us In Lines	109
For a Moment	110
Cloud Fight	111
Realms	112
Twilight Blanket	113
Cards	114
Sullen Cast	115
Making Rules	116
Color and Death	117
Hanging	118
You Cannot Go	119
Rhyme of Rime	120
Observations	121
613	122
Forest	123
Given Manner and Tides	124
The Incessant	125
A Strand of Her Hair	126
Cages	127
The Azure Asylum	128
L.A. Longing	129
Submission	130
This Final Place	131

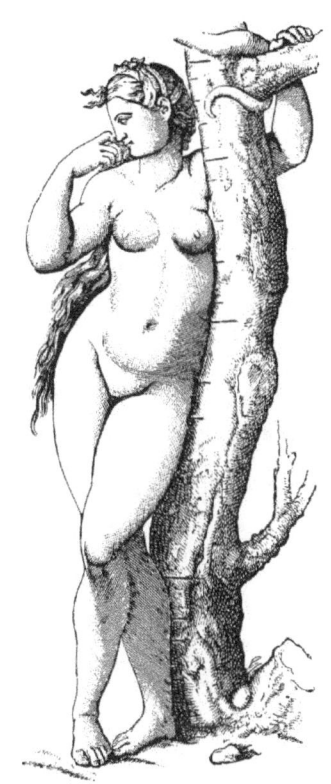

Eve by **Raphael**

Storm

stay awake for these things you must know
following snakes that enter and grow
the moon shadow dances intending you lost
far from home and knowing the cost

the answer you seek is not to a question
but a question posed to the answer in turn
no reason or rhyme in the river man's mind
choose with a word to fly or to burn

come join us all by the midnight sun
for the darkness is here, there's nowhere to run
gather round the secret is warm
thundering whispers of still nearing storms

she goes out in the rain and loses her name
comes back inside and sits by the flame
she dances in fire and shrugs off the dark
takes your mind elsewhere lives by a spark

keep Summer's secrets in Autumn's late snows
and emeralds buried in ivory rows
salvation comes only to one that shall seek
what's buried and lonely, what's barren and meek

feeling more pain than warranted seems
somewhere inside a stranger's strange dream
living out lives and turning in faces
leaving behind no love and no traces

The Shadow Lover

and what are we but unforgiven
lying under starry skies
burning like a wandering killer
filling holes we shoot inside

surrounded by a shadow lover
knife held high above her head
preaching words an age old written
hoping still to raise the dead

what you think your caution's healing
has made it sicker day by day
and as the flag its colors fading
dressed in code and in decay

soldiers stand with waiting orders
trained to target once to find
fathers hang just over yonder
mothers raped and charged with crimes

the killer here becomes our victim
the dead are bloated, next in line
apathy chasing fame and envy
nothing left of days gone by

To Cover Blue Miles

she smelled of jasmine
and tasted of wine
a sweet seduction
once over to find

begging for opulence
and words not unkind
a suitor for ages
must make her mine

blond lockets dance
in cadence to wind
tasseled and furled
reminds her of when

the sun set below
the ocean's warm smile
and her eyes cast a glance
to cover blue miles

the tide slowly churns
under moon's spying eye
she takes out her heart
and rests it on mine

with the words and echoes
of whence so far came
on her face like a king
the time and its stain

Into Your Tides

the allure your flower
apart its petals pinned
by your black-nailed fingertips
what magic lies within?

the gentle landing of my tongue
whips awake your world
tasting all that tries to hide
and now becomes unfurled

with ever growing speed arrive
harder still each time
rolling deep electric waves
taking in what's mine

quivering thighs
lingering sighs
desperate release
into your tides

Trunk

languid like the ocean's face
placid, resting, feigning grace
trip to see the mountain's peak
blocked by Satan's spreading wings

taken from what place we know
brought in chains before me
blood red sky drains its tears
the tired words from page three

Secrets and Sacred

the highway spoke
in lines and waves
out through the darkness
and into the caves

one of the mind
may follow it still
if magic to seek
beyond the next hill

secrets and sacred
soldiers and wars
finding sides to stand behind
closing all new doors

perception leading some away
in furtherance of tales
and what some written pages sold
to ships that had no sails

turpentine and gasoline
to clean the black and glue
stuck inside the ocean walls
bursting forth with blue

Until Flesh Becomes Bone

what's broken
is what never came
the dream, the angel
in death, just the same

for a million candles' efforts
showing nothing but the dark
since the bite in the garden
since the whisper of the lark

prisoners in exile
promises in vein
blood-splattered colors
held high in shame

what time becomes
but an end unto its own
wrapping lies in circles
until flesh becomes then bone

swarming like envy
held by blade at bay
nothing but reflections
on long forgotten day

Off to Grey

our minds unwind
as our bodies entwine
tangled singularity
swimming in sublime

you are my angel
and one of a kind
who knew the power
when I held you in time

broken down bleeding
your name will be mine
reticence fumbled
tried though away
thinking nothing other than
you and your day
not what you're leaving
not the sweet taste
not the moments
not the feelings
you can never replace

discourse determined
theories in play
try to kill what's left inside
quickly so to run away
far off to gray
far off to cold
far off to another
anyone to hold

Consider

whomever may remember her
in her golden light
draped with rays of loving sun
holding fast the birds of night
flutter still and finding none
but still not lonesome to seem
bequest sought, request bought
rhyming incantations
singularly dour
and souring feelings
like the springs vengeful heat
raking ivory from the mountains
breaking currents at her feet
stone paths covered
by time's weary hand
and symbols youth carved
for salvation still starved
calling out names
in dark, eerie tones
the sign of the new ones
coming now home
will you grant her safe passage?
she'll move through you
and you'll love her ghost
consider the weight
of what you love most

To Lend

something left of nothing
a song with angels dead
something left of someone
a year long winter's dread

a tale's been told on nights too cold
to find a warming friend
with words so crafted to beguile
the meaning of the end

perpetuate the darkened skies
whom hidden message send
your salvation to the dream aligned
would you care to lend?

Eternity's Chains

plagued like a river
whose run will know no end
slither still underneath
found my only friend
have and hold on
have and hold on
hard to hold on
hard to hold on
what's missing
what's missing
never found
somewhere in between
I'm all over
I'm under
I'm over
and things have changed
the price is raised
the hammer cocked
the sinner praised
singular
now plenty
and last breaths linger
for honest men
sometimes for snakes
broken by a wanting
for nothing to forsake
clean the slate
eat the cake
its burden heavy
eternity's chains

Don't Pretend

let us not
henceforth pretend
the solace you seek
is that of a friend

by your poisonous sting
I've been wounded before
you squander your flower
as simply a whore

the midnight wanders
wide in its wake
an ivory body
in moonlight to take

from the crown a jewel
from the soul you forsake
as I'm tasting your sin
like a fresh piece of cake

the day would come
the once foretold
when behind new door
the terror of old

they found you that night
alone, unafraid
just beginning to smell
in remote, shallow grave

Library

there's nothing here
I've already looked
just cascading mazes
and dusty old books

written by hands
which lived in a world
of myriad lunacy
and purple-haired girls

bound in silence
are the answers untold
minds since numbed
to the questions they hold

unknowing that death
reserves each a place
close to the heart
and fallen from grace

Brother

azure breath and cyclical steam
siphoned from a mystic's dream
open windows, wood framed minds
cornered passion, futile time

sluts in skirt on red streets tread
ghostly shadows of the already dead
houses built from sweat and from greed
the hungry eat, the brethren bleed

The Island of Everywhere

seeking seas of certain tide
casting glances far and wide
does the lonely charter of man
guide his ever steady hand

the pain would surely tear her sails
from their natural mast
and leave the ship adrift if so
for years perhaps to last

but some force of will let's say
keeps the billow firm
with proud resolve her breasts affront
from bow unto her stern

the change of days and winds of fate
may tempt a lighter hand
but solemn a man hither seen
whom through more pain can stand

the waves shall onward carry his soul
far as the looking glass may see
the island whose gates of shining gold
o'er which mortal men can't peek

Sun is Mine

sun is mine on wondrous day
took the life of waiting pray
she never did it for me anyway
and now she's gone to the Milky Way

fear is strong in those who bleed
strong indeed obtrude to feed
upon silver-skied and wretched lies
to ditch and lye the shovel heed

Birth Yet Anew

nothing matters again
as the hand becomes lucid
and moves just past ten

falling back down
as I trace its old path
counting the moments
as lonely lives pass

the darkness sits heavier
than I ever recalled
of course, I remember
the long days of Fall
crying to see the face of the cold
killing the leaves
before they grow old

and if it was one
would we know then from two
take two from one
a birth yet anew

the fate of the days
and the face of night
merged in a circle
wound much too tight

Synchronicity

nothing matters again
as the hand becomes lucid
and moves just past ten

falling back down
as I trace its old path
counting the moments
as lonely lives pass

the darkness sits heavier
than I ever recalled
of course, I remember
the long days of Fall
crying to see the face of the cold
killing the leaves
before they grow old

and if it was one
would we know then from two
take two from one
a birth yet anew

the fate of the days
and the face of night
merged in a circle
wound much too tight

Birth

it's been that way
since the dawn of day
whispers adjacent
of souls in decay

simply it's put
put simply in play
day fades to night
and returns then to stay

drunken at times
tight, twisting frames
lucid reminders
of young sultry dames

schematic at best
amongst all the mirth
to die on the vine
and miss out on birth

Far Below

had I known this would be
my own woeful fate
the corners were turned
a page just too late

the ink that's now fading
begs text to be read
before the time passing
when life becomes dead

for in the breeze lies
a secret yet still
that once can be heard
through the old windowsill

and be seen where the panes
form their true lines
where the azure sky leads
and the blackened street finds

inside to look
behold the decree
to keep outside ones
who'll not have you see

the rules have now changed
it's a game you don't know
walk a straight line
to your death far below

Ballerinas and Whisky

ballerinas and whisky
why are you here?
dying slow or dying quickly
pick a grave and go
forward thinking
backward thought
years like toast glass clinking
casually laughing
at our collective ignorance
and so we've bought
that wall is a flower
that tear is a raven
that blood is a missive
whose words our burdens bear
the other side is still
right here
twisted light and in disguise
if we only had
the ninth key
to open the seventh door
in darkness
would we swim
no more

More Than Black

she found the gun
whilst looking for friends
whose powers quite simply
would bring forth the end

her golden locks glistened
besmirched with fresh blood
the muffled sound echoed
a rock dropped to mud

now, do you feel better?
she asks in mid flight
destination unknown
unveiled by her fright

for what if the life
she took was her own?
and what's more than that
-it was simply on loan

collecting no option, or so it would seem
trapped nowhere in nowhere between
nothing on earth and nothing in dreams
as real and as shrill
as her failing last screams

the emptiness opened
a void more than black
with a penitent grin
-there was no turning back

The Devil's Inscription

for what has been born
and what has been lost
whatever called right
whatever the cost

it seems now true
in the truest of sense
for here, for this time
we sit on the fence

be there be war
be there be peace
we'll always know why
neither will cease

by faith or by fraud
by nickels, by time
all will it be
in the end
all mine

Comes Yet Still

the sutured veracity comes yet still
with whisky in hand and a promising pill
and to the tides that creep in at night
keep a secret at bay
and are born for a fight

down diagonal, yet standing right broad
a caretaker's moon still settled in fog
beams that get through
surely struggle it seems
to find a safe place
made of innocent dreams

the ebony dye of the sinner is cast
and makes its way out
not rushed, but not fast
to the non-lookers whom
should be made aware
seek to find the true light
not a simply glare

and so with these words
the door comes to rest
in earnest with favors
undone to the best
and in cycles of fire
the eternal is born
make your way now!
you've been fairly warned

Vehement Vision

solitude and serenity
night beckoned arrives
dousing day with an evil shade
illusions by which
I surely survive

an allegorical enclave
bludgeons the scene
blood and torment
fall prey to serene

this is my theater
to watch candles cry
drool down their faces
eruption am I

for closing Act Three
in climactic disguise
when the curtain opens
the audience dies

Now

lace lays lazily
seems so serene
crisp, clean, cleansing
spiraling, summer stream

darkened dame dashing
into insidious Ides
where while we wander
take tokens tide

now never nail nothing, not nothing
for five's finished - fell four feet
so sad, so solemn, so stinking sweet
who would wager when we walk?
roads rambling, regal
round ranches, real rot
nothing nascent, never not

random reconciliation registered
born barely breathing
broken becoming beautiful
lonely lying loosely
dreaming dying daily
evil even enters
without whispering why

Rolling Hills of Azure

it seemed more perfect
to the flower of morn
than the days that died
so long before

bearing still wretched
the scent of a whore
a common man's refuge
behind a closed door

in hills rolling azure
beneath watchful sky
hidden dreams still lathered
rain falls like wine

from the heavens opened
the truth at once revealed
to those undeserving
swallow down their pills

looking from the inside
the storm swelling wide
waves of towering frustration
crashing downward onto pride

Banter

dark
cunning evocation
fecundity displayed

regularity
dripping faucets
and come stains

high pile rugs
wreaked of what lie beneath
rolled like joints

smooth edges of caskets
and deep sorrows
traffic moves

and the dew is fresh
sparking on tips of blades
so many saved

and relinquishment
red lights and the smell
dampness and splattering puddles

the walls were black
dim parking lots
beams of artificial light

why was she there?
with her 24-karat hair
and her clean-shaven box

She knew my name!

Left

nothing can bring you back
to your aching hour
and with the chime
you're out of time
maybe love
will you outlast

longer than the butler waiting
higher than what fell below
tried and tied with railroad ties
left alone approaching slow

Avenue

like black ink
the rain felt heavy
the city is lonely
and broken
a whore
so beautiful
and dangerous
lights scattered like
heartache
casting dim illumination
across the staggered sky of concrete
and the roadside darkness
its damp and smelly roil
the wind picked up
and kicked foxing papers into spiraling freaks
tossed through the air like ghosts
of days past
of hope
of the now disappearing face
of prosperity and success
of a once vibrant center
of an expanding consciousness

Flying

above the raging azure seas
wings unbound we take to fly
soaring far out of our heads
leaving world and woe behind

From the Mountain

I've come down from the mountain
bringing news for my friends
in the end there is nothing
just this carnival of sin

for when days like children older
forsake their very lives
in shiny robes of blood red satin
come carnivorous elves with knives

bodies set aflame burn high
their pointed judgments right
as hammer pulls back round in chamber
time to say good night

I bid you all adieu for now
reach to close the door once more
Oh! to be one last time fucked
by this vile, wretched whore

Seems Unsettled

a query proposed - when will this end?
no more friends to beg or to lend
until the dark lives in shadows' light
a secret kept, is a secret cry

visible resting upon the hill's face
a map of sorts leading to the next place
in my relinquishment of love left still
with vengeance born but yet to kill

stabbing pains the memories bring
sinister guest buried deep with a sting
forever and once and never again
it seems unsettled, it has never been

Promised to Whom

and so the promised land
this ravenous existence
pained with the driven pangs
of decadence by restraint
the mind mislead, unfed, bleeding
left for dead

sea of regret in which I here swim
not knowing why I just cannot be
left unfixed henceforth broken down
with only eternity remaining to see

slid around underground, underfoot like me
for what is left of a soul who's seen its own demise?
and to the soldiers holding guns
to judge with their own eyes

there is no escape from the walls that hide
the very unsettling truth deep inside
if anything else to me becomes wise
let us beware twisting knives of their lies

to what extent do I thus proclaim?
to those who've done me wrong in this game
boasting with smiles and masks at their sides
seeking a man in a boy's simple eyes

so is it mine? this burden be held?
with hands in bloodied time
who is to release the chains
encased within my mind?

And It's Over

down her thigh and around her back
seeking a cavern of warmth and safety
where I may retreat into seclusion
and explore

point of entry slowly avails
welcoming inch after inch
for nine or more miles
her eyes alight with fury and sin
sequestering defenses
to deeper let in

pressing our breaths
together in one
synergistic and high
exhalation's cry!

wiping away tears
her lips peak a smile
her flowing hair resting
a tasseled, mane of red
her hands gently caress
the lines of my face
her heart bleeds silent
with a genuine grace

like none yet I have known
in these miles of life
I won't forget
when I held her at night

Drenched

there is light in the dark
of the black lodge
masks and stars
aprons and bars
finding ways through
inequity's veil
drenched in the
afterbirth of
thwarted redemption
and safe harbor
they are here now
and gather
conspicuous
and naked
smoke
fire
desire
irons

And to...?

and what knave?
to whom beholden?
this night
her hair so golden
as to send the furthest ship
a glimpse of yellowed flame

and to what love?
surely betrothed or close
as if her lips to God
his design relished in repose

words have ne'er been spoken
thus worthy of such a face
glimmering on this barren sphere
as if no one else was here

if your weapon be laid down
prepare to yourself to fight
you heart a battle 'til the end
to win her or forsake

clever cliffs
cast a shadow
as long as day lives on
and what a man
caught in the dark
desires to sail on

rocky reefs lie like hidden snakes
under flowing azure sheets
waiting like a dragon lair
to footsteps near he waits

Is the Tragedy

Love is trickery
and blame
a heavy burden
laden with guilt and
insufficiency
faces and games
lying and truth
the same
what poor soul
must need such
hollow
relief
masking only
that pain
they cannot mention
realize,
or present sans disguise
no one ever really knows
anyone else
and trying
is the tragedy

Atop Married Hill

kicking and thrashing
her flower is born
of greed and lust
a crown without thorns

the chemicals spread
like her legs for a dime
bringing the feeling
illusion sublime

and down from his perch
he gives a quick stare
he's back inside now
wondering why is he there

at home his wife sits
with worries unstill
and holds his name high
from atop married hill

her hair flung back
with a sigh much too late
for he is up and around
collecting cash for to pay

for something that's nothing
he's struggling still
as the look on her face
wants him back
and he will

Eager Soldiers

as if to say this vapid life
like drain to beckoned sand
coagulating memories
like soldiers gather land

in thoughts of maze and haze gray days
lie secrets pharaoh seek
though not before a mortal heart
shall her wet lips spread to peak

This Cage

your reticence
plundered your innocence
tied now to the bed
pussy full of hard cock
denying your temptations
has burdened you
into wandering pastures of confusion
and lucid reminders float like
stubborn clouds marring the perfect azure
that illusions reign this plain
and destiny like none other avows
simply to allow you to be your own
like the indiscernible droplet of water
cascading down like a twisting snake
through the emerald forest
lost in the swell of the raging water
shattering against hardened rocks
and lying lazy on soft-soiled shorelines
this cage

The Ghost and The Insane

night staggered along slowly
across the wide ocean-carved line
sun having just perished for the evening's remainder
toiling elsewhere until its forced morn rebirth

while adjacent death and life mingle
seemingly aimlessly
over grove
mountain and mire
concrete and conifer
rooftop and river
bound for the decaying door
of every living man

notwithstanding the hollow efforts
and futility of an inherent denial
hours will take back
what is rightfully theirs

surrounded by nothing but moist, black soil
remembered like a falling leaf in Autumn
in lonely rows of forgotten souls
leaving only names etched in stone

pleasantries abated by the causes of the day
for what's on the next step, stay out of our way
puzzles and pictures of fables and fame
chasing a ghost and finding insane

Behind the Face

disgrace lies behind the face
honest heart you're bound to break
bring the fire, throw the stone
sending hell to heaven home

words mislead the honest man
while the killer knows the game
too much time a soul to fill
burning trigger feels the same

I hear you scream and brass fall still
a decision rang aloud
single shot and what she willed
now buried in the clouds

in the dark the black disguise
whispers death and wonders why
what an odd game to call a name
when summer comes to die

in the springtime of evolution
destruction of what's to come
beggars chose to wear their chains
and rich men beg for some

This Empty Room with You

there's a bounty on my heart
one too many lovers
when things fall apart
we're left with no other

I hung stars in the night sky
painted over what you didn't like
I set myself on fire
when you wanted light

why satisfy me?
if you're leaving me soon
there's nothing I need
in this empty room with you

we might always be what we want
but can't be this is anymore
one and one is four
in sum, I'm out the door

Pink Moons and Blue Lagoons

I met a few people in a dream
with whom I intended to keep touch
never did get their names
they said it wouldn't matter much

she must choose before the leaves fall
for if no choice then nothing at all
the mist covered the mountain
and she found me there waiting

strange winds from the west
whispering we are what's left
of freedom and of grace
and of this vast, empty place

so take what you must
and be on your way
find pink moons and blue lagoons
scattered across the Milky Way

Sailing

and whom this night in fastened throw
battened down like sails
into the storm of ecstasy
impassioned, wrangled tales

one of love and one of lore
which shall bear the fruit?
cast upon the crown of waves
tossed in vile pursuit

dirtied skies and killers' eyes
lurk in din and dim
into the wherewithal and still
buried deep within

Wondering

I am the words
you are the melody
nothing more is true
I will spend a thousand years
making one from two

I am the sun
you are the moon
nothing less is true
I will spend a thousand years
shining light on you

how do we allow
the story line
to get confused?
life gets in the way of us
one left then
from two

here and there
miles afar
take the memory away for now
but leave it in my heart

And Just Run

tepid resurgence of forlorn thought
I tuck it away so it thus might be sought
seemingly sultry though breeze still abates
to face unforgiven salvation awaits

a garden whose seeds bear sin on their own
torn from their stems left to die all alone
reaching to grasp empty hands of the sky
trading their thorns for wings and to fly

morning will come like a young man at sea
curled in a corner of dark, unwed dreams
bring forth a woman to guide his mast true
picking her poison so carefully choose

and silly to some it may seem as it cries
who'd never born witness to such wicked lies
presenting as fathers in devil's disguise
casting their judgment with black soulless eyes

then truly to seek something laid true
I ask a man, so ask only of you
we are alive, can it not be so said?
alas, we are living amongst walking dead

so, toast us now! as time grows old
beckoning penance and calls to be sold
nothing shall stand in the way of the beast
steadying calls for a hasty retreat
sacred hearth burns with fire of sin
I beg of Thee to trust me quick friend
through the hottest flames of the crashing sun
take your soul - and just run!

Meet Again

Grace
slipped off her lace
and stood
to the mirror
face to face
taking in
all of herself
like none other had
certainly no man
except for him
and with sunrise
lament for her
transgression
sets in
though both imagine
in stars
and in dreams
that she will come home
but they will never
meet again

Once Were Far

dancing like a stalking wolf
'round the scent of flesh and bone
knowing now if so to choose
either way we'll all be gone

a penthouse and a basement
the killer and the saint
a vacancy is lingering
that never goes to waste

from the ground I see a star
from heaven can't be seen
hanging shadows once were far
like me stuck between

Shopping List

morning sat and waited
for something else to come along
midnight pain is growing weary
words just come out wrong

vigilance gives no surety
that betrayal can't unwind
never knowing what beholds
the corners of her mind

allured by her magic box
secured then by her kiss
found inside a dark, wet dream
where reality is bliss

I hung the moon
I held the sun
I tamed the wind
I am the one

bleeding, broken
hearts and souls
seek something sacred
still growing old

she'll wander on another
and find fair-weather end
feelings led away by lies
always moving never mend

Nothing Saved

shadows seek solace
in Summer's sparse shade
and the fresh broken-hearted
try to roll back the days

but with each falling hour
the skies move their ways
and find resurrection
where nothing is saved

waves raked against the sand
extricating the unfocused back to sea
leaving the rooted to make a stand
make a reason now for being

Waiting

so many lovers, so many scars
black sky-scattered battlefield stars
hills filled with fire won't scare me away
from your beautiful magic and chemical rage

Hollywood nights
how did we survive?
on the edge of alive
like Bonnie & Clyde

gilded cage battered
still searching for gold
swimming in fountains
we never get old

don't get confused
this is not about you
I'm dealing with the feeling
that I like the abuse

your love takes hold
like well threaded noose
I won't hang around
just waiting to lose

What Garden

what garden is this?
above the din, the serpent's hiss
the direction of the soul
so misleading
what to question?
when the answer is bleeding
like a stone
patiently waiting to be thrown
in its own private hell
sequestered alone
flying high
with wings untied
clouds stained
by ivory glow
blood red killed
by velvet night
and come your dreams
and one you seek

On Owning Sunset

on owning Sunset
my mistress, evening dame
streets cleared before me
ghosts knew my name

the hills burned in tribute
the lonely came around
I took them as I choose
and left them loosely bound

in that blissful time
mysteries comfortably lie
Chateaus and sofas
endless drink off the vine
and love held sublime
twisted tales, off the rails
details lost in rhyme

red or blond
both tasted so familiar
streetlight vagabond
drive to be inside
always stepping back
in shadows to hide

A Scene at Riverside

the seraph sat stoic
gun in her lap
cold and unloaded
but not thinking back
peering across the onyx waves
touched by the rippling tickle
of a silver moon sliver
identifying with a flash
each crest's face - a lost soul
washed over and forgotten
like last Summer's lover
a tear fell unnoticed
from her bright
violet eyes

The Sick Men

the sick men
walked the hallways
in soft-soled shoes
seeking out young boys
unawares
in uniformed skits
diamond-patterned
black and white
like the eyes of death
corridors of filth
sweeping range
and the buffer
or reality
staircases through levels of hell
alone
fleeting and fleeing
word smithing salvation
from the sick delusions
of faulty pages
glass doors shut
with a slam and
are chained after 5:00
know when
to run
find a phone boy
tell your story
make them back off
and retreat into
their moral insolence
and condemnation

Stones

there were no directions
no pictures on rocks
no voice in the darkness
to shepherd the flock

children wandered
where trees once stood
where neighbors smiled
and only meant good

now the wind blows
and changes a mind
nothing's in stone
since lost in time

Between Her Legs

as the door shuts tight
and she closes her legs
she rolls to her side
and in silence she begs

to whomever can hear
no matter how far
heal these wounds, sew them shut
leave the scar

she won't forget
and she'll make it well known
she makes them smile with skills
thereby well-honed

and as morning wakes
with familiar pains
she lets go of the horse
and rides with no reigns

as evening closes
that day of her last
will she miss the missteps
of the unforgiven and past

innocence lost
just too early it seems
maybe she'll wake
and 'twill all be a dream

Red Sun

there will be no lost
there will be no winner
no matter the cost
skies hang under One
decided once and done
bring thou death
or bring thou fun
laid to rest
under red sun

So

and will the same
with words become
the prophet so I seek?
from scars on knees
and hearts behold
as heavy as are meek

I've dug graves
you'll never find
think again
if speak your mind

who holds the gavel?
who holds the scythe?
dealing in death
the power of spite

Too Real

night peeled itself open like a ripening flower
unveiling its presence with a sensuous smirk
casting hope to those caged its towers
who writhe in regret and draw fancies in dirt

dirtied faces
bloodied seams
salvation wasted
too real it seems

wicked winters strangle
summer's proffered whores
ships a-sail cast a line
and off to yonder shores

Nearing Insanity

I was unsure of my whereabouts
other than being inside of her
which felt more like home than
any actual street address

she was tight, and I watched
as I pulled myself out
taking her cherry red wrapper with me
tightly wound around
she comes with utter cosmic intensity
again
and again
22 that night
until we had to stop
give her vehement
declaration
of nearing insanity

Left Alone

the reluctant vigilance
the heavy burden
of something so strange
and unrelated
it somehow made sense

night poured over his soul
like an ink well spilled over stark white paper
and insanity was only a word
people whispered
in corners
about anyone other

their own hands bloodied
by cruelty, indifference, or is there one
you vile hypocrites!

the bell rang
but there was nothing
the kitchen sat empty
like a forgotten grave
adorned with withering flowers
and the stale memory of love

sounds echoed in silence
off the fading walls
of lucidity
and the blade is sharp
like the pain

Let Her

let her show you her way
where the shadows hide
where the secrets play
let her be a mystery
which captivates you mind
let her be a secret
hold her longer than there's time

Leaving Only Time

Summer came
and Summer went
she'd become more elusive these days
seemingly shorter night
one of each echoing too closely
to that of yesterday
when the slow rapping of the waves
on the rotting dock posts calms
and silence becomes of the faces
mountain tops conspire
to destroy all other places
sharing secrets with
the lingering passerby
threshold bearing
unleash to cry
and thunderous roars
as heavens violently shake the skies
like ill-tempered parent
to disobedient child
not love
not love
but frustration
and confusion
we are lost
like the clear, spherical reflection
of the sun on the flat, calm lake
when the water begins to rage
and disorientation and deluge
combat the acrid staleness of
the sublime
and disrupt the order
leaving only time

Waves

what you thought was real
has made you seem a fool
broken by a loving hand
when kindness became cruel

and with the steady ocean flow
the cresting mighty wave
rising to its fullest peak
you wonder if you're saved

for the power of the mind will fall
when challenged by the heart
nothing done and nothing to
send away - just fall apart

Everyone's a Whore

a reckoning is beckoning
from over yonder hill
the battle won and now the fun
with drink and colored pill

souls subside beneath the din
and finds her no surprise
her long blond hair and sultry curves
beset by sea blue eyes

the evening parted on good terms
intact with devil's smile
knowing still the darkness left
in the minutes and the miles

for the real truth lies
behind closed black doors
where none had been before
with new names
and masks adorn
everyone's a whore

The Lonely People

the lonely people
who want to belong
the lonely people
who only feel wrong

the lonely people
who are walking in line
the lonely people
who are sad all the time

an empty pillow
or an empty soul
which is next to them
who else can know

so smile
when you see a frown
and maybe turn
a dark day around

Id

I am
I was
I stay
because

I am lost
I am found

I am light
I am fire
I am death
I am desire

Quiver and Yonder

considering the verses
opening the words
assuming nothing but what's meant
gathering the herds

useful tools for leading fools
latent mines afoot
acquiring nothing in return
smoking pits and soot

over yonder carvings root
labors former told
viscous cycles spin in blood
equal sums and sold

Nights & Fire

her hair was fire
her body was sin
her bite filled with poison
her taste led me in

Hollywood off Sunset
a place secrets keep
secrets of their own
in blood and in sheets

black can be darker
when in the name of love
I'm a man of the hours
I'll take you from above

finding new places
so far inside
upon their discovery
you can't help but hide

run as you might
and find you again
you see how this goes
and how it will end

An Even Number

she possessed a certain...
antiquarian lament
a soulful drudgery
so heavy-laden
with the reflections
of skeletons
dragging drying bones
across the mist-draped
misshaped
and incongruent boundaries
of countless lives
a discourse
never resolved
a resolute fervor
never dissolved
stained with the fallen
and painted by prayer
cloaked and forlorn
arriving never there

Whatever

The breeze abated rather suddenly, like the freedoms that abound in the endless summers of youth. Abated abundance as it were - the innocence lost and the reluctant perspective gained. Though not to be presumed any more attuned to what *is* being than the inherent fleeting and unrecognizable astuteness in the wisdom and smile of a child. Chasing wind through corridors of a maze, whilst directions yonder made to follow, to many so unclear - that a life is merely an attempt, however successful, to discern the will and word as their named is called through the cream.

Still Sour

just leave me alone
but please don't go
without these chains
I just can't know

becoming soon nothing
what I should be
everything other than
you want to see

and in the darkness
your demons awake
bring friends and fire
truth will forsake

in the waning hours
time rolls to a stop
as lingering life
turns still sour

When

I'm enveloped by purity
of love and of sin
forgiveness sits on the fence
thinking back to when

summer was flying
clouds were in hand
nothing but beginnings
no clothes made of sand

Eternal Sea

and to whom the written ones
cast aside by the ink of ignorance
and the light of time passed
unearthed and reborn
sewn shut and re-torn
left behind in the punishing waves
clearing now the mist of haze
making seen the virgin page
and louder still the echoes cry
for salvation from the fables dry
and whose time may come be it yours or mine
and does not seek, not sought, we find
and worlds that lay upon our feet
empires strong, new faces replete
and if it's right and right is wrong
the tunes they played in those old songs
hold still inside the harmony a key
to oblivion's ship and the eternal sea

Lies Still

the birch and the maid
the winter sting
and summer fade
breathing still
what lies, what's made
in dreams
and in that place
the one in the dark
forbade

A Morning View

The morning moved swiftly, passing people by like a silent freight train, hauling the cargo of their dreams quietly past, undetected, as they molt in their cast-iron oblivion.

For recklessness not tolerated in the winds that fill the sails, and society's skipper sprinkles the dust of complacency over the eyes of the herd - now calmed by fear and the trepidation excised - namely that of choice - and its certain pain.

Horizons painted with careful detail, exacting to leave nothing to doubt and nothing to the inane imagination.

Sweet Taste

she'd never thought of herself as a whore
she drank alone and then closed the wood door
evening pinched with a pain so well known
to what man hast given, for her to be shown

she tires quickly and gives way to the night
awakens abruptly when touched in sheer fright
to find no one there, but knows there had been
perhaps akin angel who'd wagered on sin

she'd conquered the fear made it stronger in turn
by allowing her dreams on the pyre to burn
stuck the wrong medicine in the right wound
wound up floating in watery tomb

as the crisp chill bludgeons
night's weary face
her heart astill begins
set on her last chase
for in void of the ether
a new friend awaits

Flames

it's much too late for saving
it's much too late for grace
it's much too late for reasons
time to start digging graves
words that seemed like truth
echoed over solemn hills
like the eagle, like the sun
flying free, held by no one

what man can hold a stone?
and therefore call it gold
what man behold a boy?
and say ye shall ne'er grow old
rivers of dissidence
rivers of blood
curling through what's left of her
and winding up in mud

nothing there of greener pastures
they wait in circles over blue
hoping then to turn to red
then shine with hope like you
sweeter than death
larger than life
black like the eye of night
buried still
far out of sight

mourners come
and gather names
lighting candles
citing flames

Building Skies

you left
and the universe
fell down all around
this funeral pyre

so I'll pick up the stars
one at a time
and staple them back
up in the sky

And It's Over

down her thigh and around her back
seeking a cavern of warmth and safety
where I may retreat into seclusion
and explore

point of entry slowly avails
welcoming inch after inch
for nine or more miles
her eyes alight with fury and sin
sequestering defenses
to deeper let in

pressing our breaths
together in one
synergistic and high
exhalation's cry!

wiping away tears
her lips peak a smile
her flowing hair resting
a tasseled mane of red

her hands gently caress
the lines of my face
her heart bleeds silent
with a genuine grace

like none yet I have known
in these miles of life
I won't forget
when I held her at night

Armada

she harbored
ships with holds
full of gold
and sent no letters
so none be told

whilst hidden
by the azure seas
breaking still like
early dawn
and secrets
yet to keep

finding solace
in billowed sails
whispering winds
warn of coming gales

pledged to none
just course set true
she's come about
and coming for you

Certain Pain

it's a certain pain
you just can't place
but one which resides
in only one space

the ritual death
of a seven-day dream
hot pecan pie
vanilla ice cream

plunging and surging
thrusting distrust
comes to an end
love buries lust

tears emancipated
heartbeats return
midnight beers
hot grease burns

The Death of Dawn

She settled in
much like an unwanted house guest
uncomfortable yet too tired
to pack her things
and walk back over
the black hills
from whence she rose
buckled down in time
watching wardens
wishing wantonly
wondering what wickedness
belies her blood red skies
death sits weary
staring at the ground
just across the boulevard
from where she was found
he hadn't had the heart
to take her soul away
like a child
and his favorite toy
with which to play
he liked her mystical breezes
and colors of her dress
but alas! hours still pass
and she must die
die at last
but not by his hand
for he is gathered
and turns away
disappearing
until another day
for now
settled on elsewhere prey

(cont'd)

shortly thereafter
her countenance is washed away
as if by a luke warm tide
on the tidy, cool sand
she is murdered
by the liquid blue backdrop
rising slowly as she burns unawares
and dilutes her fecundity
as slow ivory gumdrops
make way across the azure canvas
mysterious as the black sea
its dimensions hidden
its crimes so discrete
the changing face of
the graveyard of dreams
tossed aside by frightful storm
falling back upon the heart
the heavy stone of fate
shed the body or shed the mind
which will someone else soon find
and bury deep to cover sin
never let the whispers in

The Outsiders

the outside always felt right
not desired per se
just better than the alternative
- them
boxed in reliquary
of ancient dreams
and pale reason
to no end
but destruction
and mediocrity
never knowing
the key

A Virgin's Thighs

the day parted slowly
like a virgin's wary thighs
breaking through the hardened night
giving way to blue surprise

mountains fall in line
like soldiers snapping to
quick to judge and quick to find
inside her welcomes you

moist and warm, entangled forms
tower large above the hues
vicious circles sure to form
as defenses become unglued

for in her hallowed chambers
deep and open wide
a pause, a breath, an open hand
begs you come inside

as if the seraph's trumpet sounds
with perfect time and place
her tasseled hair and tangled mind
pushing still the pace

at last, a wave, crashing down
euphoric into shore
pulls out slowly into dark
from whence it came before

Faces Now in Mirrors Wade

behind the empty walls you hide
the secrets deep inside
from what becomes these days
decaying sun and empty life

a whore would fare much better in
the darkened halls of night
sequence filled and aces played
to not die out of sight

and will the burrowed memories
still the notion once retained
of smiles born of vengeance
and the lives of those and lame

for what's been left of nothing
once a man now crowned a king
of something promised will it come
a betrayal thereby stings

and colors born of blood that runs
as deep as oceans still
adorn the skies of children's' dreams
and sunsets left behind

to the take the promises broken
now and days and days ago
born of times of sorrow-born
and sorrow-born they go
through the days having shamed their own
and scurried time away
faces now in mirrors wade
into the depths of the unknown

Self-Affair

it's the prison
swooning dames
scenes re-played
ah, the dirty games we played

mindless sheep led by greed
planting mindless, heretic seed
into a world of illusion and dust
an opulent cake frosted with lust

maze alluring
weak succumb
to the evil of day
their name, a sum

iconoclastic retreat
into snow covered hills
induced unconscious
where reality chills

eyes roll back
like a carpet and close
too late to turn
blackened face of a rose

Dig It

degradation
contemplation
seclusion
illusion
halos
hailstorms
shivering
stuttering
prayers
falling
salvation
stalling
forewarned
fair-weather
fiending
incredulity
floating
dead
burrowing
head
womb
tomb
trip
skip

Sepulcher

the pale evening
and the angel
merging

indignance
they'll try to take
from me

you'll find
nothing here
agendas seek
victims
and the allure
of power
born of greed
and malice aforethought
notwithstanding
intent
genuine or otherwise
ink to flame
bears repeating
following footsteps
carefully placed
to form a riddle

doors with no keys
you shall meet
and fall from
every height to which
you aspired
in your false light
bury it
deep

When What Wake

I will wander on
through haze of days
looking for light
in the wrong place
shadows seek solace
where man leaves
no wake

Lost Time

intent on making nothing of the situation
except for the singular point

of redemption

you won't speak my name
anymore

your betrayal holds fast
once again

walls creep closer and
pictures look less familiar
they used to cry
and they will rest in flames
thieves have removed their hearts
thinking they were gold
holy wars and tombstone tours
vapid reliqy and truth beseech
forewarned by hidden words
pages damp with tears
I can no longer be
not with this emptiness
when I stare in her eyes
there's no one there

The Spy

the girl across the street
sat by the window and cried
Oh! to know the reasons
and comfort her inside

the afternoon dwindled
but my focus still remained
knowing nothing of her
aside from just her name

summer's solace fading
like the light behind her eyes
if she only knew the way
she moved me each and every night

Stealing Repose

I laid in bed beside you
even though you were gone
I felt your breath
landing gently on my bare chest
where your face once
softly rested
in repose
no one knows
what demons lie
behind what's shown
and I burn
and I own
this crown
and I will change
the heart of every man

Clocks

the clock's hour hand
like a relentless shovel
at six digs down
into my soul
then moving to twelve
throwing dirt
back up over
its two o'clock shoulder
digging up your memory
over
and over
and over
again
when
will
it
end?

Your Death

do you remember when you died?
or maybe you survived
the new parade was quite the sight
lingering whispers you're still alive

we're at war today you know
with what's held back and what's in tow
secrets, serpents, twisting time
hiding still the venomous crime

Who?

lately I'm not feeling like myself
have I forgotten?
or am I someone else?
no one's there
when I call my name
if you are - take pity
quit this cruel, harsh game

whispers slip through sleeping trees
no quarter here
have I forgotten?
have you misplaced
breaking free, seeking sane
to bring to knees
the one that came?

stow your mercy
light your flame
find what's wild
born to tame

Sunday Night in Hollywood

what you call this I don't care
lost in your long, black cherry hair
ripped up jeans, tight black dress
two locks on the door, revolver at rest

I drove home later naked
hair wet to stay awake
past liquor stores and movie stars
past the lions and the fake

your taste stayed with me
on through the night
I missed your
your sweet and bloody bite

Ritual

death had come like a stealthy layer of fog
night was blissfully unaware
caught in the reflections
of the bygone day
the moon hung low
in pale red blood-soaked regency
delicate and violent in its precise articulation
of the eternal
and cascading throws of bounding light
from mountaintops along ridgelines
and seascapes
vigilance echoes
warnings and secrets
like the wind time will end
though waits for no one
except the dead
captured and treasonous
any hope befallen to the dark
drained of its last tricks
and devils and sages
angels and pages
seek to save the sacrilege
of the earthen being
in its natural state of assured ignorance
and desperation

For a Time

ah, sweet temptation!
what were you exactly?
before the written page
your birth decried
with black ink and dye
on souls cast wide
darkened doors
now whisper in fear
of who may come
or who may hear
of plans to reap
other than what man
has cherished fine
bringing still the fires
since the dawn of time
were the days more simple?
were the words more kind?
was the judgment more balanced?
were the sun and moon a crime?
breaking soil finding stone
alas we become dust from bone
into the air to fly again
with wings spread wide
and eyes alight
oh, glory!
we are indeed
alive
alive!
alive?

That Was Then

she said 'I love you'
with tears in her eyes
while I was inside her
it was the first time
then she rode me
and came again
it was early
and I can't remember the time or day
but we woke up for more
she wanted me to come inside her
but I wouldn't
and then slept
the sun rose in this
unfamiliar place
somewhere off Wilshire
light peaked in through the tall window
illuminating the recent vacancy next to me
she was making me breakfast
I found her again on her birthday
years later
I was out on Sunset and rang her bell in Bel Air
she answered
and asked me in
and then took me in
it was years before I saw her again
then a few more
and she laid out before me naked
then a voicemail
a few more years
an email
and that was then
do they know your name now?
do you remember your words?

Standing By

for what has been or comes to be
what's born of the solemn fruit tree
held by the sky and the air holding fast
standing by waiting a savior at last

casting shadows from distant suns
holding its burden while tempted to run
not of this blue, not of this fight
under pale ivory of midsummer night

Such Affairs

desire or consolation
you'll never know
by the look in her eyes
wrapped in disguise
laid out before you
tightly guarded surprise

can this happen to you?
you may not think so
such beauty and treachery
pure as the fresh fallen snow

you'll only discover
when she's changed her name
such affairs
no burdens hold
just time and toil
the young become old

Creeping

creeping echoes
hallow cries
shallow grave sites
where beggars lie

split by iron
bade by stone
made by magic
secrets roam

dropping hints
salvation's play
key to finding
so pages say

blood and wine
tales and time
pain and suffering
end sublime

names erased
tombs encased
night fell last
no more day

She

she bit her lip
in a beguiling play
to get me between her thighs
and come inside to stay
knowing not of the depth I'll take
and the parts of her
she wished not awake
for in the twilight
her ignorance dwells
with tinkering tales
and haunting iron bells
snickering still
as her pillow flat lies
biding the time
until time bends to die

They Kept Us in Lines

they kept us in lines
and watched
one step, one step
they chanted
like the insane

they kept us in lines
ants marching seaside
cascading over the emeralds
beset by an incorrigible innocence
and writhing
in soulful disillusionment

they kept us in lines
perverted
hot and straight
in the coarsely humid air
of a summer
marked by
torture
insult and ruin
bring me a letter

they kept us in lines
and now
they
die

For a Moment

for a moment
I held the wind
her name escapes me
as she did then

for a moment
I held fire
her name is whispered
below the din

for a moment
I held the skies
her body laid before me
oceans in her eyes

for a moment
I held forever
for a moment
she was never

Cloud Fight

the clouds fought each other
for the attention of the horizon
much like girls over a boy at the bar
whom they wish to fill vacant holes
or vultures rabid and furious
over freshly-made carrion
never knowing why
but desperate oh to be
the apple hanging proudly
on someone else's tree
regret may closely follow
in many cases next
the hunt beats the kill
and yet on and on
and round and round
always on the ready
wander still

Realms

it's over, but it's not done
it may be buried, but no one's won
it's coming again, it's at the door
no matter saint, heathen, healer, or whore
painting pictures on blood-stained floors
creeping silence, no keys, no more
whispering somewhere locked tight inside
the four crumbling walls of your mind

flying not quite the notion
while the seven stir the potion
knowing nothing of what's at stake
burning fires, will to take
deceptions linger
'round murmuring din
swelling still louder
growing with sin

strangling sabotage
the formula's wrong
slowly it opens
the journey so long
into the fold
into the black
into the realm
of no turning back

Twilight Blanket

a twilight blanket
a broadcast death
a cresting wave
a young girl's breast
a night unwound
a wound new found
a tight rope bound
a secret she's held
a burden proving heavy
a heartache like a crime
a broken promise lingers
until the end of time

Cards

equal parts of heaven and hell
buried stories still to tell
in darkened corners meet again
knowing this will never end

are we not but one and same?
burning under sky-borne flame
turning back no trying might
fate of hands played in the night

Sullen Cast

brilliant light
brilliant lies
keep them all
deep inside
quell the dark
its hidden sides
thousand years wide
outshined
rooms of processed lies
living never died
bury not wantonly
bury not fast
tend to graves
raise the flowers
rake the memories
steal off to caves
dripping, stillborn
hallow and eerie

Making Rules

smoke-filled anterooms
where they make our rules
in fancy dress
and fancy jewels
breaking news
drawn by scheming hand
imagine the blood
dripping to sand
taking print for truth
by ink they're sold
just fools
chasing glitter
while hidden is gold
repeat the line
wear the mask
survive the ritual
perform the task
you will be told
the word
of a man

Colors and Death

Death held the door
and for the first time
realized its impatience
as it stood steadfast, and weary
yet anxious to get on with
what lies ahead
its guests caravaned from the sea of black vehicles
headlights stretched into the distance
like a row of candlelight mourners
enveloped by the drapery of low lying fog
and the eerie blackness that seemed
of no color at all

Hanging

she lays down next to me
mellow and naked
her cool, silken skin
still slightly damp
gently touches mine
and comforts me
inside
my mind
as our bodies slowly
entwine
until tight like
the ropes of
a noose

oh! how I love that feeling...

You Cannot Go

bleach the stain
remove the pain
suffering beats
driving down rain

temptation reigns
revolution suppressed
boredom's whore
is so thus depressed

found bare in sorrow's
wet, narrow cave
she knows time will turn
the worst of the knaves

bring to her offerings
to spike her blue vein
grasping her neck
painted word reads insane

the sting forces her
away from the pain
to a place
she said
you cannot go

Rhyme of Rime

with crushing blow the serpent fell
abrupt to Satan's side
then cinders of the fire cast
to dance a mile wide

into the sea of vapid sin
a smile thrown too far
eternity in settled dawn
now draws as black as tar

and writhing in the mellow twist
a maiden fair as true
a servant of the page's beast
and stirring quite the rue

voices raised and anger swells
to meet the bar set high
in red rains of hell be drenched
thus never to get dry

Observations

due to the recent happenstance
a vacancy between her legs
I was eager to reengage efforts
at winning her affections
she sat stalwart and proper
giving no indication of interest
in any of the activity flurrying around her
or any notice at all of the swelling din
her peach lips
her porcelain skin
she moved me like a tempest
across oceans of sin
her simple skirt billowed
in the gentle summer breeze
revealing her long, smooth legs
perfection at ease
shifting her weight
held high on black heels
is she truly real?

613

violet violence
vaginal vogue
raging radiance
hallowed holes

sweet sweat soured
heated, hanging here
finding forthwith frenzy
taking token tears

with wanted worry
waiting warriors wane
until usurped urgency
paints pursuant pain

tumult taken tricks
peaceful placid plains
bloody barren bodies
sorrow's solemn shame

The Forest

three hours
and she came
black-hooded
on mounted steed
third rider
the same
quenched the riddle
leaving the morrow
seemed beguiling
seemed so much more
the forest lamented
in its canopy majestic
hovering over
torch-lit flames
and spotted fires
rituals beneath
words they speak
blood rite of the ancient
secrets still to seek
purple hazes
mystic winds
changing faces
erasing sins

Given Manner and Tides

vanished in the hallmark haze
love leaves seldom a trace
like a clever murder cleaned up with bleach
or the death of a message
scrawled in the sands of a beach
taken by tides who hold the secrets
you seek
bartering with eternity
for only a peek
of what lies beneath
may show you the way
how to live above
throughout bloody day
and standing right hollow
misery depletes
black eyes and quiet sighs
epistles held like
bastard child
in darkened corners
where whispers belie
given manner
and time you will die

The Incessant

her olive skin radiates with gravitational sequence
her lips tucked to one side peaking a sinister smile
they part slightly so as to cast
the breath of uncertainty my way
her spiraling pools of mahogany set behind
darkened liner and drizzled hair
with the sheen of a summer tide
begging me to come to come inside
to start anew with bluer eyes
wider stance with jet black skies
time twisted, twisted time
a see through lie, sun-washed mind
and strictly thought as you bend a knee
take care to take it deep or so the string would say
pillow first then four fingers to slide
come now girl in me confide
the sins that thrash through the swamp-like thoughts
of dwindled flames and kindled dames
the sinking ship and battened crew
from the deck the storm alight across the mighty miles
of azure tips and crested souls
who beg still with
oblivion reviled

A Strand of Her Hair

the small cabin sat perched
quiet, intentional
amongst the sunburst foliage
its idle surroundings still formidable
against the harsh coming winds
and the death of winter
raging fires roar
in desperate hearths
keeping warm
desperate hearts
wanting and holding
playing then folding
set back and step forward
finding a door once open
no longer there
floating like an angel
in the later April breeze
a strand of her hair

Cages

I'm gonna break these chains
and fly again
drive the nails through
the endless nights
the hollow clouds of sin

she's in a cage
and that's where she'll stay
no matter the face she wears
under rainy skies
there is no day

ever rain, ever pain
the solemn single sold
drowning still in empty lakes
held by years of old

The Azure Asylum

this is my pain
nocturnal vigilance pales
leaving the darkness to be
insanity's playground

stabbing memories
steal the air from my lungs
restricting the spirit inside
from its natural inclination to flee

as the day rises, I fall again
betwixt the intersection of realities
and their incongruent boundaries
which ebb and flow like a spring delta
eventually emptying its soul
into the depths of
the azure asylum

L.A. Longing

and now she sits
under idle timber
and its sparse, collective canopy
as the clouds cry
for her mistakes
and she still wonders
why
as tears and soil dry
like the years passing by
hard to recount
like the hand I hold now
was it her in the prophecy?
cold winds twist and howl
she wandered too far
from the warmth of the dream
too late in realizing
it was simply meant to be

Submission

she'll paint the roses on my grave
but won't say my name

she's on her knees
begging not for salvation
strangling what's left of life
surrendering nothing

does she even care?

not a sweet submission
her long blond hair
a braided, twisting noose
will I ever get out of here?

do I even care?

in the end we always lose
stepping out of line
to step into play
lost behind where nothing withers
hiding something
hiding from someone
shadows give you up
string you up for fun
stuck between circuitous routes
knowing each
will surely bring about
the tale drawn on tattered page
what's the message?

can anyone show me?

This Final Place

single light
hallowed night
wolves to howl
bitter cold bite

cloaked in black
a hooker's proud lace
still the flame's crackle
and silence to waste

leaves crunch underfoot
make way through the maze
of ancient tall pines
adorning this final place

sequestered by martyrs
beholden by kings
laden with legacies
soothing with sting

mysteries lingering
words never said
until the moon's phase
aligns with the dead

www.ingramcontent.com/pod-product-compliance
Lightning Source LLC
Chambersburg PA
CBHW051805040426
42446CB00007B/534